The Words of Others are All We Have

A Poetic Conversation

by

Louise Machen and J Daniel West

First published 2024 by The Hedgehog Poetry Press,

5 Coppack House, Churchill Avenue, Clevedon. BS21 6QW

www.hedgehogpress.co.uk

Copyright © Louise Machen and J Daniel West 2024

The right of Louise Machen and J Daniel West to be identified as the authors of this work has been asserted in accordance with the Copyright, Designs and Patents Act 1988. All rights reserved. No part of this publication may be reproduced, stored in or introduced into a retrieval system, or transmitted in any form, or by any means (electronic, mechanical, photocopying, recording or otherwise) without prior written permissions of the publisher. Any person who does any unauthorised act in relation to this publication may be liable for criminal prosecution and civil claims for damages.

ISBN: 978-1-916830-02-8

"Dedicated to the bread on the bus stop. Long live the bread."

Contents

The Estate 7
Wild Boars 8
Mornings are Wiser than Evenings 9
Hometown Magnification 10
I Stand Outside Your House and Try to Remember 11
Jar in Hand 12
Dirt 13
Even Underground 14
The Underpass 15
Knowing Your Lot 16
The Escape 17
The Iron Trellis of Eden 18
The Piccadilly Gardens of Eden 19
Prince and Pauper 20
Northern Quarter 21
I Can't Decide if the Graffiti is Art or not Because I Can't
Determine its Intent 22
This Graffiti is not Art 23
Affirmations in Black Marker 24
Homecoming 25

Acknowledgements 26

THE ESTATE

High-rise glass, stained with grime, sieves the light
into spaces of systematic indifference
where carpets and skirting boards never meet
and we repeat this curtainless continuation:
staring out of windows into a delirium
of life beyond uniform blocks, the corner shop
and the back of the chippy.

Watch as eight-year-old babysitters
dip a dodie in their bag of Kali
and cross the road between prayer and plea –
careful not to tread on the cracks
of their precarious existence:
heirs of Thatcherism and a rented inheritance.

Patience is no virtue when waiting for death
in this box within a box within a tower
hidden behind a fobbed door; coffin space in the lift
a reminder of our exit.
And we're told this is liveable by those who don't breathe
the heavy heat of pre-pay meters, fuelled by fettered sleep
with only caffeine in the bloodstream.

Press your hands against the windowpane;
take a look through the confines of urban decay
where ambition is soiled by time.
On our estate, the meek are left nothing
but shards of glass they've chiselled away –
trophies claimed from trying to break out
and into a world not made for us
from a house that someone else built.

WILD BOARS

Out beyond dusk down identical prefab roads
where the only way to know which one you're on
is the graffiti street sign sprayed on the side of a house

Play a game of Odd One Out,
count the terrace rows and try to find the one
with an occupied house, newspaper curtains
taped to glass - a rare zebra sighting in a savannah
of plywood boards over empty frames

Jumpers piled on uncut grass give us
early exposure to moving goalposts
while the other is repeatedly painted on a wall
below a disregarded No Ball Games sign
where the brazen culprit thuds hollow against brick
to the raucous applause of sirens and helicopters

Weathered wooden panels and rain stained concrete
sprawl through weeds like a root network,
spreading from our mother watching over us
in the centre of everything,

but it's only a matter of time before she, like the rest
of us, will be stripped to the bone before collapsing
under the spiteful pressure of her lost potential,
joining her children in an entropy as inescapable as her walls,
even as they come down so completely around us

MORNINGS ARE WISER THAN EVENINGS

The kids are playing Kerby in the street,
their sounds bounce between terraced homes:
canticle of Sunday mornings.
Uneven paving postpones the play:
      "Let's go down our end instead!"
Hubba-Bubba gets spat into the gutter
and the chorus of complaint takes off
avoiding a buggy that skirts about, its tenant unwashed,
hair full of lugs, content with peeling the wrapper
from a Vimto lolly and sacrificing it
to the wind.

The kids are playing Kerby in the street,
the ball bouncing between terraced homes
signifying to all that morning has broken
like the bottles that provide obstacles on the overgrown path.
Play is suspended by a familiar refrain:
      "You lot should play outside your own house!"
The killjoy curses the ditch-laden tarmac
and they give her the Vs as she marches away,
tacitly affirming they will remain unmoved
staying clear of the door where last night's commotion
has now grown silent.
Unwanted everywhere, they play on regardless.

The kids are playing Kerby in the street,
their rows resound between terraced homes
breaking my sleep with adult language:
      "It's my fuckin' ball! I'm tellin' yer mam!"
Arguments loiter between unwelcome light
and the comfort of cold bedding.
The endless call from outside grates at this peace,
bouncing through the letterbox,
off the uncarpeted floor and into the cocoon
where the word "mam" is having a lie-in,
where mornings are wiser than evenings,
and I wish I'd have popped that fucking ball.

HOMETOWN MAGNIFICATION

There's no home left in my hometown.

The only house I ever knew has strangers
tripping over the creaky step,
listening to the boiler hum
in the corner of the bedroom,
pulling their dogs away from chewing
at the fibreglass panels in the kitchen.

Looking at the house on Google Maps
there's a car in the driveway
I don't recognise

But the street view picture is old,
and I see a familiar *Beware of Dog* sign
        on the fence,
and I see a familiar basket hanging from
        the wrought iron hook out front,
and I see a familiar white ball that - when I wrote on it -
        made my mum see a ghost,
and I see a familiar collection of ornaments on the living room windowsill
        beneath a familiar tasselled blind.

I spend time in that one spot
spinning the camera to see everything I knew,
from my earliest memories
to flying the nest,
from learning to ride a bike
to coming home drunk as dawn
peaked over the rooftops.

I think about how I'll never see it again
and how it belongs in the hands of someone else.

I STAND OUTSIDE YOUR HOUSE AND TRY TO REMEMBER

His Singapore shadow spills from a green door,
over red-brick coping stones, into the quiet road
where I approach the past of a Northern lad
who barked in Japanese while children slept.

My photographs are other people's memories
of this cobbled street when I fit into the crook
of his arm held by the scarred palms
he would press down into the window ledge

thick-framed glasses gazing at the garage
its awnings red and white – painted like half
a rising sun. *It's in his blood*, she'd say,
like tattoos made with the pin of his Pacific Star,

Sunday naptime, dripping butties, hands in pockets,
pints of bitter bought with her housekeeping money,
hateful voices, Double-Dutch and no rice pudding.
His presence lingers like the scent

of other people's freshly washed belongings in the sun –
this place he would fire all his guns at once
exacting obedience with his dog-eared prayer book
lined with notes of things he wouldn't talk about.

A voyeur and collector of third-hand stories,
I join the magpies with their military salute
to collapsible and sunless memories –
somewhere lies an elegy, but not here.

JAR IN HAND

I never understood that name,
painted on a battered sign that swayed
in the wind and waved enticingly at children
on the playground across the road,
beckoning like smoke
curled into the shape of stained fingers
that spoke of impossible promises.

So many of us never made it farther than that sign,
swaying in time with its shadow
holding onto an unnamed anger with stained fingers
trying to keep pace with the cracks in the tarmac
suffocating under the vast expanse of the night -

only to find themselves returning
time and again to the place they hate so much,
the only place they ever really belonged. And when
the stars, too, return to the steadfast holds
of their murky vantage points
they watch the men who choose not to
watch their children play in the school yard
a stone's throw from the battered sign.

The last time I set foot under that shadow
was for the wake of a man
who never would again. To avoid ripping out
my heart a thousand times I stared at the walls
and fell head first into their contradictions

History clung to each curling corner of brittle paper,
previous lives leaving their mark
in a way that was anything but nostalgic
and turned the present into an off-coloured lie,
pressing layers into each other
in a way the future will ceaselessly pine over.

Outside, in the sunless afternoon, I squint at the
battered sign's stained fingers
beckoning its next generation

DIRT

This dirt on my knees is ingrained in the creases of my skin.
You don't see it? Look closely. It was ground in
behind those child-like eyes

where black capillaries spray a winter sky.
Hair on damp earth – mossy and paralysed.
Fed-upon. Dirt-covered. Wordless. Still.

See, if I were to peel away the years, exhuming soil horizons,
layers of gritty filth would spill like marbles uncontained;
buried in nonchalance, the colour of memory fades.

Don't let my blue lips bother you, at times I forget to breathe –
but these burrowing insects, beneath the encasement,
remind me they are still alive in their sempiternal state.

Sorry, I'll get dressed and put this all away.

EVEN UNDERGROUND

She walks the long way home from the bus stop
relishing how the handles of the carrier bags cut deeper
into her fingers because these are the only marks
she's allowed to choose to put on her own body.

She stops and rests for a while where moss breaks
through the stained-glass concrete slabs in the
most abundance and reclines until the yellow weeds
form a vignette like a pinhole narrowing in on her.

She meditates, almost, closes her eyes and listens
with jealousy to the misplaced seagulls that
will get to leave once they're done circling her
headstone adorned with someone else's name.

She climbs the stairs of her mausoleum with her
elbows aching from apprehension, her fingers
purple and throbbing, and even though she knows
each ascent brings her undoing, she can't turn away.

She looks out at the graveyard diorama and decides
one day she'll keep climbing, because once she makes it
to the roof the seagulls can have her and at least then,
in their greedy bellies, she'll finally make it out of here.

THE UNDERPASS

This tiled tunnel is the only way home
(unless you want to walk all the way around).
Its synthetic lighting pollutes the night
streaming out onto the pavement
like Uriel shining out into the darkness of sin.
But this is not a light that signifies salvation,
it is a sharp-sighted spirit that welcomes you
to take a closer look at the stains on your dress;
how the patterns on your tights are back to front.
Those evenly spaced luminaries will expose the truths
of early evening, asking questions about knotted hair –
that measured choice of underwear.
You know how your make-up will look
below the fiery swords of light boxes in enclosed spaces,
but this tiled tunnel is the only way home
(unless you want to walk all the way around).

KNOWING YOUR LOT

Is it so enviable to believe yourself the righteous man
in the eyes of a vengeful and petty god?

Were your anonymous daughters afraid
when you offered their bodies as bargaining chips
in place of his holy enforcers
to curry favour within the status quo?

It's easy to walk the streets
of Sodom and see sin
behind the eyes of every passer-by
when your metric for morality
fits comfortably in the palm of your hand

It's easy to walk the streets
when you believe judgement will come
and will be made in your favour

It's easy
for you
to walk the streets.

When the time comes
for fire and fury to fall from the sky,
and we who dared to be anything other than
subservient
in a strangling system
are forced to repent and beg forgiveness,
you take no qualms in fleeing
because your subservience is almighty

And when your anonymous wife
beholds a moment of pity,
regret, perhaps,
she is punished for daring to look back in sympathy,
a pointless gesture left too late,
but you do not worry
about that feeling
overcoming you

THE ESCAPE

Don't look back upon the ruin;
the ache for familiarity will pass
like hunger pains of the past
and sunsets of multihued bruises.

Make a new home elsewhere;
fill it with potted plants and sin –
don't fall back and into him,
into his patient, brackish poisoning.

Rip new grass from the ground
and bathe in the wrong side of midnight.
Oil the throat that wouldn't speak
to arm your tongue with greasy freedom.

Keep running for the hills –
go beyond the pink at the edge of the sky
and its roseate plea: there is no comfort
in the fire and flood of nostalgia.

THE IRON TRELLIS OF EDEN

Look at this sanctuary,
        this Eden he has given you.
Smell the aroma of this veritable garden
        that blooms in every colourful scent.
Taste the abundant cornucopia he has
        graciously provided for your convenience.
Feel how your nakedness
        keeps you free from shackles.
Hear his words and how they strive
        to guide you towards happiness and safety.

Indulge a thirst that will never be quenched
and a hunger that will never be sated

Believe the lie when he says you're full

Don't question how he uses your nakedness
as a shackle with those beyond the fence
filled with shame under their clothed,
judgemental bodies

Don't question the fence
because it keeps the wickedness out
because it keeps you safe

Don't question how the vines and climbing ivy
wind their way through the chain links
and obscure the world beyond,
because plants grow around a trellis
just like he told you

THE PICCADILLY GARDENS OF EDEN

"Hell is empty and all the devils are here." - William Shakespeare

Concrete ramparts observe this postlapsarian patch
once bedecked with geometric flower beds
edged neatly by trimmed grass and cherry blossom trees:
an ornamental sunken garden that filled with sunken people

over time and, in time, these stone benches on threadbare turf
replaced roses and tulips, like Primark with Lewis's; no longer
dug into the core of the earth, a flat plain of lawns turned to mud
from corporate greed and a flood of Mancunian rain –

a jet-wash would go a long way. The toothless face of abandonment
sags behind bare-footed children playing between fountain jets;
steeped in inertia, indifference and piss, they are somewhere other
than this, open-mouthed, searching for euphoria away from here –

all eyes open on the grounds of an old infirmary, an old asylum,
but this is the era of self-medication and poison is plentiful.
Cans of Special Brew are knocked back beneath magnolia trees,
entrenched in the scent of cannabis where shopping totes

filled with vagaries pass people whose plastic luggage is about to burst
with the filthy remains of a life that only exists when the visual cortex
reduces activity and shoppers are ballerinas dancing with snakes
winding around the tree of life with their already knowing.

There is nakedness here, but not the sinful kind:
souls bared on pieces of cardboard bleed into the pavement
beside betting slips laid on a blanket – no need for tea or coffee,
doesn't know what he believes in but offers pieces of his life for nothing.

A statue of humanity circled by two-toed pigeons feasting on the leftovers
of leftovers in this antipathy where man is but a living being and above it all,
a preacher with a sandwich board damns us all to hell if we continue on this,
our path of wickedness – as if we've not been there already.

PRINCE AND PAUPER

High-rise skylines leave naive minds wide-eyed
but the space that splits a spire leaves them wanting.

Great glass erections claw their way to the heavens,
Towers of Babel filled with countless silent tongues
while across the way, decay and disarray slouch
weather-beaten and grey, stained from the rain
but I know my way through the concrete maze.
We are not the same.

We are only the same
when perceiving our faces from a safe enough
distance, as close as denial will let you believe
your triumphant comfort is choice over chance.

Streets away and worlds apart, the space that splits a
spire starts its steady march to sweep the sins down
into the stretching chasm. Thrown stones fall short
of making art and instead slowly form a fortress
with ramparts pulled from the pits of granite hearts.

The game is zero sum. Every sun-kissed monolith comes
with the glass facade of gentrification, maintains its goal
is to reclaim the run-down and bring about a paradise,
looks with shame on the very vices it vows to tame and
once again concrete pays the price, swept under the
rug and out of the frame, ignored until it goes away.
We are not the same.

NORTHERN QUARTER

Mooching through alleyways past midday
on a Sunday, I avoid pavement cafes
and their out-of-town-brunchers.

They wander at their out-of-town pace,
lugging suitcases and shopping bags
and happy-hour hangovers
as I thread through this side of town.

These back-street cobbles are comfortable
beneath my Converse –
worn and moulded to the shape of me.

I pass this picture of tall stunning sadness:
face raw, tears fresh, wearing last night's
gold dress, hole in the foot of her tights,
heels in her hands, following a man

who should have been left behind.
I stop a second, but change my mind –
when I was her, I wouldn't have listened.

Friends take confessionals below the branches
of a silver tree overseen by colours of the palace
where advice given in pavement cracks
is a common voice I forget to hear.

No one guides my ear or my arm
just these streets taking me the way I've always gone
to places I have never been.

I CAN'T DECIDE IF THE GRAFFITI IS ART OR NOT BECAUSE I CAN'T DETERMINE ITS INTENT

Inside an alcove
a man uses his only coat
as a sleeping bag,

curled up to tuck
his tattered shoes away
from the elements.

Outside a trendy bar
freshly opened
three doors down

a group of loud financiers
paid hundreds of pounds
for the same look

and with no sense of irony
mock the rough sleeper's
inability to afford such couture.

THIS GRAFFITI IS NOT ART

                        it is guidance on the back of a cubicle door
screaming **THINGS WILL GET BETTER THAN THIS** under lyrics
by The Smiths: *heaven knows I'm miserable now* scrawled again
and again, that black pen defaced by the kindness of strangers'
philosophical statements: Oscar Wilde's *gutter* a communal favourite
(repeatedly misquoted in unheard conversations).

This graffiti is not art; it is a cry for help with replies unseen adorning
the back of a purple bus seat next to opinions about *Dave* and penises
of worrying shapes. These honest words of escape share lives
of a different font on a similar route – echoes of youth
in marker pen hearts cementing a friendship, imagining stars
and forevers – the things we once believed in.

AFFIRMATIONS IN BLACK MARKER

Words scrawled on the walls of a toilet stall
wrap around him in ways he'd never find
in the lofty heights of the sanitised glass
cubicles on the outside looking in. Vandals

validate him anonymously, conveying a
sense of community, as if they knew exactly who
would - one day - stumble across these affirmations
written in black marker, opulent flourishes

next to hasty scrawls where someone short
on time still had a desperation to make him
aware he had people on his side. He reads the words
aloud, stands and delivers a sermon to save himself

before spilling from the pulpit and its broken door
out into the arms of his saints and lovers to hear
what gospels they have at the ready because,
he knows, the words of others are all we have.

HOMECOMING

The door opens and I enter,
disrobe myself of a fabricated world;
leave the dirt of outside
unbooted at the welcome mat.

The petrol can of petulant independence
is long empty, scorch marks now faint
in this hallway of repentance. A beggar
who can't be a chooser, life on castors

rolling back to familiar phrases in the mouths
of strangers, where my outstretched hand
will often be met:
one room, one chair, one brew.

We are washed and sanctified
in the poorly-decorated living rooms
we were once ashamed of –
humbled by the *good* biscuits on each return.

If we're lucky, we don't inherit kingdoms
but the words of voices that read us to sleep
who absolve us of our childish negligence
where we never had enough, but always will.

ACKNOWLEDGEMENTS

I want to acknowledge those who have been constant in their support of my writing journey. Whether that be extending me a platform for my work, being a listening ear for draft after draft, sharing my poetry with others, offering a kind word at a reading or casting an eye over edits. Thank you. Your honesty, time and encouragement offer me shelter from the fair-weather friends of the world: your words keep mine flowing.

Louise Machin

To everyone who heard versions of these poems before they were the paragons of perfection presented here, and to everyone who is yet to hear them. To everyone who gave me a page or a stage that led me here. To everyone who lives these pages, know you're not alone. To my partner. To my family. For my dad.

J Daniel West

"Set in a vivid landscape of urban decay, a brutal Eden where paradise isn't lost, it was just never an option. These 'conversation' poems rise above their beginnings like a plume: part smoke, part accusation and part defiance and without sentimentality into vital poetry written as a remembrance and as a warning to the rest of the lifestyle obsessed world that we were here and some still are."

Jack Caradoc 4/10/23

"With relentless "fire and fury", this uncompromising pamphlet of poetry centres on issues of social, economic and cultural deprivation in Manchester. The poems, which highlight poor living standards and the "gritty filth" of environments, also focuses intently on adverse life experiences and lack of opportunities of an underclass and working class struggling at the edge; all the more tragic because of the gentrified communities around these poor estates – the distant "sun-kissed monoliths" of new housing development, which sharply contrast with poverty-stricken neighbourhoods. In focusing on deep inequalities, the two writers in the collaborative work shine an uncomfortable but necessary light on the grime of neglected areas and the insurmountable challenges people born without privilege face in trying to break out of the poverty trap. This no-holes barred account, rendered with sharp poeticism, makes gripping reading."

Matthew M. C. Smith, author of The Keeper of Aeons *and editor of* Black Bough.

"*The words of others are all we have* is an aptly-named pamphlet, as each poem perfectly speaks in conversation with one another in a way that harmonises in a beautiful melody throughout.

The pamphlet is a delve into gritty urban settings honeyed with nostalgia but sharpened by hindsight, and we are warmed by personal moments of exploration of both what constitutes as 'home', and the relationships that define and refine us from those places. From synthetic underpass lights to rows of Primarks and John Lewises, there is an acute ache of familiarity, along with the throb of a home altered beyond recognition.

These powerful poems will leave the reader bathing in that 'fire and flood' of yesteryears long gone, leaving the inevitable question; where does that now leave us?"

Scarlett Ward, author of Ache *and Founder of Fawn Press.*

"Urgent, vivid, and important poetry from perspectives that tend to be silenced, grasping, among other things, the entrapments of poverty, and the slipperiness of memory."

Dave Haslam, writer, broadcaster and DJ